S.O.A.K. and W.E.T.

stories of a kind
and
whispered erotic tales

POEMS BY:

TNLMNQ

DEDICATION

This book is dedicated to my grandparents.

R.I.P

TABLE OF CONTENTS

INTRODUCTION

I grew up with encyclopedias in my bedroom. I read them. I visualized. I dreamed. I drew pictures. I created, and I wrote "stories that rhymed." I figured I'd become a song writer, or a screenwriter, my pen just flowed. Writing was my release, my self-expression, my self-advice and my memory bank. At a book fair in the 5th grade, I bought a book titled, "Selected Poems of Langston Hughes." My life literally changed, and so did my writing. I discovered **poetry.**

These poems are based on true events, and true thoughts. We all think, and we all have a story behind our thoughts. Some of us just have a way with words.

This is my way.

stories of a kind

Let it **S.O.A.K**

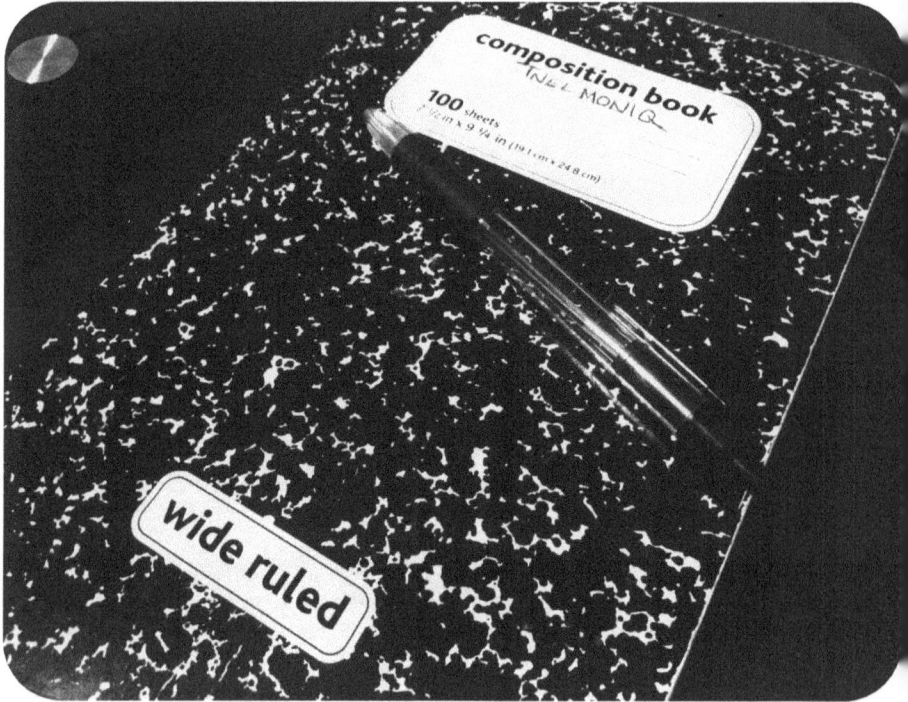

REBIRTH

I wanna get deep but I can't find my depth

I wanna breathe but I can't find my breath

I wanna speak but I can't find my voice

I wanna make a decision but I can't find my choice

I wanna think but I can't find my mind

I wanna read but I can't find my lines

Pop in one of the best documentaries of all time

For inspiration, searching for motivation

My selection, Tupac's Resurrection

Right around the corner a few blocks away was the scene of his murder

I wanna continue but I feel I can go no further

My thoughts are dismantled, my vision appears dim

My life I can't handle, my chances seem slim

I wanna take you there, but I cant find my way

I can barely describe what I feel inside, I believe it's called pain

My loved one is no longer here, he was taken on his day

To be relieved from these ground restraints and up to a better place

I wanna just live but I can only see this birth

Of the biggest fears of my life, as I continue with this search

I'm afraid of death, so afraid of death

I have so many things to accomplish and so many things to see

But being a witness to "HERE TODAY GONE TOMORROW,"

Is taking the life out of me

So I picked up the pen and applied it to this pad

To surface what's inside of me and these thoughts that I have had

Facing my fears, facing my fears

The ink on this paper smears from the drops of my tears

I sit here reflecting on the title "poet"

When I ain't picked up the pen in years

Pushed away, "back-burnered" are the invitations from my peers

The fact that my blood lay cold is hurting my heart

I never thought I'd react this way being so far apart

Instead of mourning our loss, we have to worry about funeral cost

I have to keep functioning, I have to stay strong

But some people's fate in life, just seems entirely wrong

I have never felt the way that I'm feeling before

When my grandmother passed, I knew she wasn't in pain anymore

This is different, my biggest fears have been ignited

But what I'll do is, use my strength to fight it

My pen on this pad, is my therapy session

The events of this life, I use as life lessons

Facing my fears, for things don't always appear as they seem

I just have to live through their spirits

Continuing my path, pursuing my dreams.

I WILL

Frequently underestimated, but always strong minded

Continuously educated, with experience behind it

Determined to overcome life's obstacles as they are real

I Will….

I will stay open to opportunities

And learn from life's scrutiny

I will use my experiences to my advantage

And accept that money not be spent, but managed

I will stick to my word, as a rock sits still

I Will..

I will follow through with my goals

And overcome the odds when life takes a negative toll

I will not be affected by the negative criticism

Constructive will be accepted in all forms or systems

I will steer my own direction in life's path

And be thankful for the things I already have

I will prove myself to myself, and myself alone

As I walk up the mountain, of life's stepping stone

I Will…

I'M FINE

How you doing? I'M FINE..

I think that question is sort of over-rated

Because 75% of the time, I'm NOT doing FINE

I mean, gas prices are outta line

My pockets barely got a dime

Trying to get rich but still on the try

And just the other day, I got hit from behind

What if you ask me "how I'm doing" and I really told the TRUTH

Hell, how my cell phone ain't on, "shit, SPRINT GOT ME again for real"

My home-girl be like, "nah girl, YOU GOT SPRINT, you didn't pay ya bill,"

What if instead of saying I'M FINE

I told you I was living paycheck to paycheck

Sometimes barely able to pay that

I'd give you a couple dollars, but I gotta getcha next time

What if instead of saying I'M FINE

I told you I was fuckin' with a punk

My mother's being a drunk

From neglect, to intoxication off that wine

What if instead of saying I'M FINE

I told you I was strung out and depressed

My job has got me all stressed

That fat direct deposit was a mistake that money ain't mine

What if instead of saying "I'M FINE"

I told u my lil sister was 14 going on 29

I can't quit this dude but I'm steady tryin'

Kinda stuck on stupid, think I done lost my mind

I know he ain't about shit, and I'm just wasting my time

Couldn't change my dollar wit 3 quarters, a nickel or 2 dimes

My momma all up in the business, cause you know she like to chime

I'm thinking , your dude has a gambling problem, why you all up in

mine?

I wasn't raised in the hood, but I'm steady on the grind

I'm steady looking for things, that I know I can't find

Seems like I can't get out the hole, like I'm always in a bind

Makes me wanna just rob somebody, commit some dumb ass crime

Got 3 dollars in my pocket, my car on E and the gas is 3.69

And it's car registration time AGAIN and I have NO ends

Make me just wanna NOT even drive

Then some got the nerve, to ask ME for a favor

Ain't got nothing on the gas, but always need a ride

Then offer me something to eat, which is oh so sweet

But my car runs off of GAS, not burgers and fries

And as far as that car registration is concerned,

Well, you know how that goes

I'll just have to turn that "6" into a "9"

But then to top it off, at work, when I got off

Somebody parked right next to me in a space this got-damn wide

And I know I'm skinny and all, but come on dawg!

I couldn't get my car door open in that itty bitty space if I tried

So I sit and wait, had to be at class at 6:50 and its 8

Hungry cause I didn't eat lunch on my lunch break

And he finally come move his car from that space

But only for me to find

That after fidgeting with my purse, thinking damn is this some sort of curse?

I look in my car, I had locked my damn car keys inside

Then my mom calls me on the phone, like "what the hell is going on?

Ya cousin in Compton was wearing a white Tee, got shot, almost died"

I'm thinking, is this some sort of dream or are these things really as they seem?

Because I just wanna go somewhere, close my eyes and cry

And this may sound strange, but this bum ask me for some change

I gave him all I had, because I'm just too damn kind

Because this life is really no joke, and I'm not one to smoke

But sometimes I just wanna go sit somewhere and get high

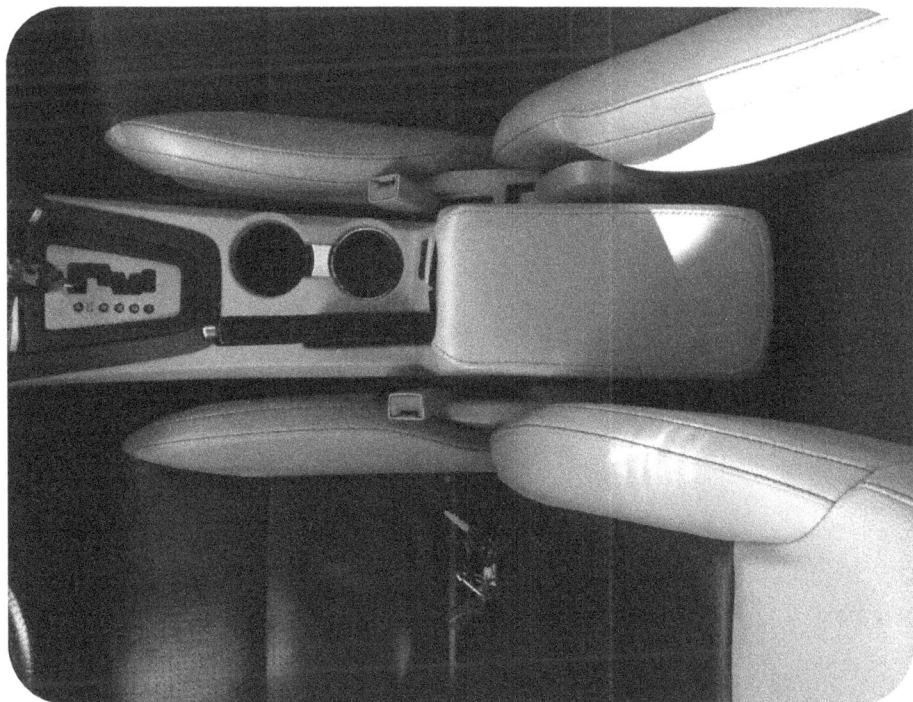

Debt stacking up left and right, bills laying everywhere in sight

Make me wanna holla like Marvin, or act like Ray and just be blind

And to tell you the truth or what's really going on

I could use a shot of patron with a little salt on the rim and a side of

lime

So as I'm walking in the mall, minding my business and all

Window shopping at things I can't buy

Instead of telling the truth, or using some excuse

If you ask me how I'm doing..."I'M FINE."

EVALUATION

Let's evaluate you from various different angles

The Timbs, the jeans, the tank top, the Kangol

The teeth, the dimples, the earring, the fade

The lashes, the eyebrows, the potential for braids

Smooth complexion, style selection I'd say size eleven

The limp in ya walk, as if you needed a cane

The stroll in ya talk, as if you were flying a plane

But, while we're on talk, exactly what are you talking about?

Can a woman hear something educated, something more than your

intensions to her body route?

How about your past accomplishments or what your future plan

holds?

Or where your mind wanders to, or what your imagination unfolds?

How about a sensual conversation, without sex in thought rotation?

Or how about you let your mind drift off and my words be

motivation?

To offer the deeper meaning, than what fronts on the exterior

Because once attracted to this being, I'm now inclined to the interior

But, to find nothing but emptiness, leading to hallow

And the bits of substance maybe found within, define themselves as shallow

Has the traditional courting routine expired? When was the last time you've had real date?

And none of this coming to the house, kickin' it on the couch, that's that shit I hate

I know if the evaluation tables were turned, I wouldn't mind fixing you a plate

I know if I stood in front of wives, girlfriends, or even average females they could all relate

And even though we all hate to admit it, we know about that

"Why you gotta be here, it's getting late..."

But all I'm asking is, for much more than what is obvious to see

And I have defined all that I can define

So lets blossom, from the inner beings of you and me.

REPRESENTATION

The tone of my skin, the texture of my hair,

The size of my lips, the gaze of my stare,

The shape of my nose, the stance of my pose,

The width of my smile, the clothes of my style,

The height of my size, the weight of my prize,

The ring in my tongue, the breath out my lungs,

The pitch of my voice, the consequence of my choice,

The color of my eyes, the talk of my lies,

The watch on my wrist, the width of my hips,

The juices I leak, the words that I speak,

The attitude I engrave, the hair before I shave,

The hands that I use, the fragrance that I choose,

The feet that I walk, the mouth that I talk,

The things obvious for you to see,

Are only outer elements of the representation, of the inner me...

Look Deeper.

HIGHS & LOWS

You fill me up and then you empty me out

You give me so many thoughts, feelings, and emotions to write about

Would it be the right decision to just let you go?

Forget about what we had, put it in the past

And keep my feelings on the low?

Throw out the photos, contacts, and sweet past times

Erase your number, stop sending texts, and stop checking mines

Forget about your presence and grab myself a rebound

Consume myself with that, even when you ARE around

Fooling myself is what I'd really be doing

It seems like no matter what happens

These feelings can't be ruined

Or should I put myself out there and protest the emotions I feel?

Ignore what people think, because I know this love is real

Confront you face to face, ask you what's the deal

Contest the added space, this break, my heart won't heal

Explain to you, I can't go thru, these emotions that you steal

Call congress, campaign the votes, I'm not gonna pass this bill

What's the deal, keep it real, I can't take anymore lows

Tryna heal my heart, mend the pieces, it can't take anymore blows

Just be up front, what are we doing, it's not just me, no one knows

I'm no longer satisfied with subjecting to the, "whatever just flows"

I'm all cried out, almost all dried out, unsure of the route you chose

But can't get past the feeling I feel, my face in your presence, it glows

So let this love manifest… let me start by giving you this rose…

LOVE YOURSELF

Those who give, seem to seldom take

And those who take seem to seldom give

Now is this any way for a human to live?

I trip off the script of typical human life

How men seem to make babies more than a lady a wife

And women, on the other hand, some of us ain't right

Tripping off subliminal things, turning maybes to mights

We focus on more material things, to escalate arguments to fights

Sweatin' on the has beens , and if nots, stressing out through the nights

Confused about the simple things, not knowing wrongs from rights

Using little things to bring tempers up to new heights

When in reality we need to just stop stressing

We seem to think it is our job to teach our companion their own lessons

So don't always over-react, hold in some of that aggression

Because they'll just think, as you got weak

3 hours later, that it was all bullshit while you sexing

But I know, I know, it gets hard, and sometimes you just gotta settle

for that

But just focus on you, and not let useless actions distract

You from what you need to be doing, whether it be

More education, preparation, or increasing your wealth

Because happiness lies beneath the surface of you first, loving

yourself.

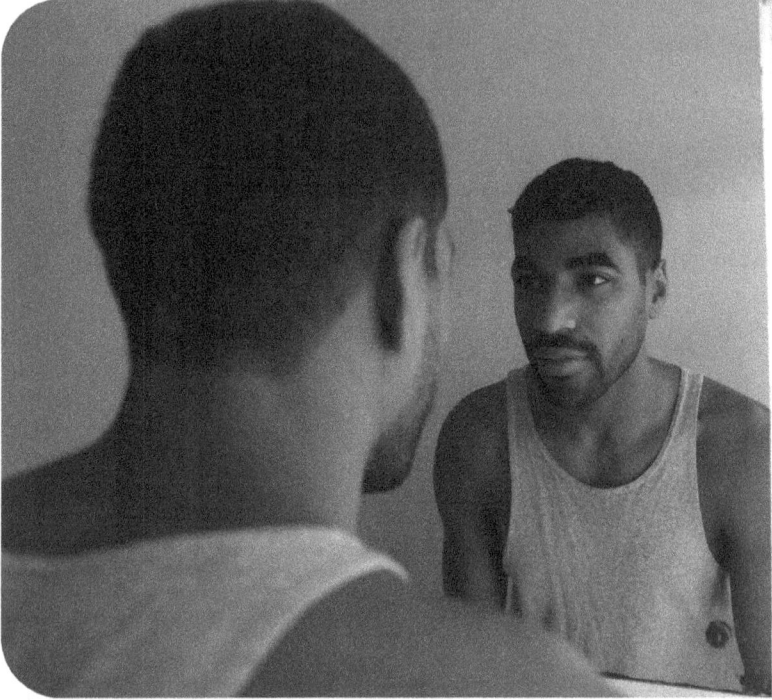

IT

Some of us define it, some of us don't

Some of us deny it, some of us won't

Some of us try it, some of us fake the funk

Some of us believe in it, when others live in doubt

Yet some of us live deep in it, and don't really know what it's about

It has existed as man was created on earth

And the two created to live it, disobeyed to never find its worth

It is stronger than any being and can stand the test of time

But when only lived through true meaning, leaving all odds behind

It is given, felt, and often taken away

It is relived, cherished, and nurtured, often giving strength to live

another day

It is sometimes misleading, deceiving, and often purposely planted

It can be perceiving or cheating, or even taken for granted,

It can be in a gesture, a writing, or even a thought

Or a tone, a speech, or a gift that's been bought

It can be horror, or a nightmare, or as fake as it seems

It can be a fantasy, a one night, or a scene in a dream,

It can be born or killed, or lived through a spirit,

And although it can't talk, it speaks loud when you hear it,

It doesn't smell, but its aroma can leave you blind,

The clouds will clear away once freed from its vines,

It can be felt through surface touch, or deep inside,

It can be pulled too much, or pushed away by pride

Even those who've been through it, can seldom define what it was,

But IT, only knows what IT is, and IT calls ITself…

LOVE.

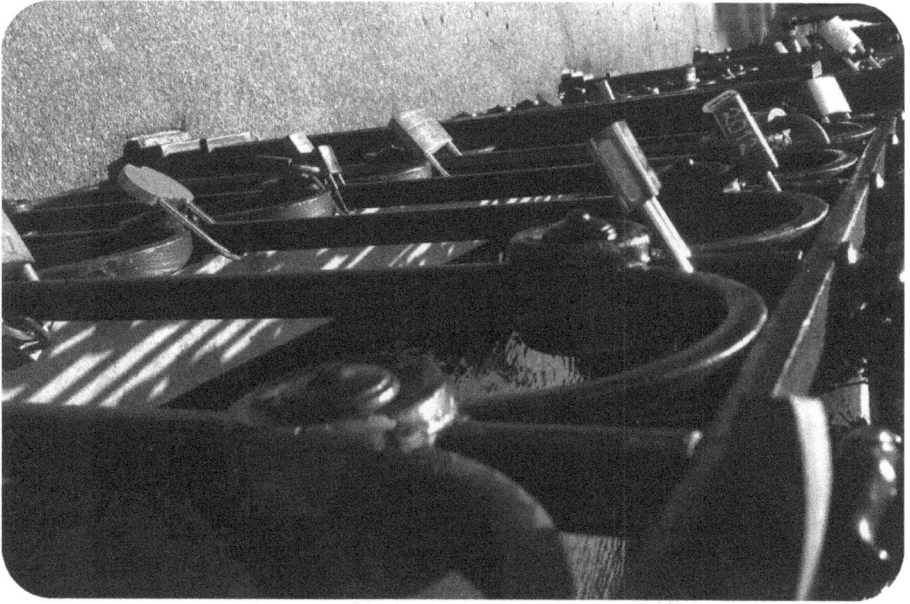

LOVE IS 2-5-4-3
(A-L-I-E)

Love is something I have previously discussed

Deviously distrust and mischievously combust

No one can really define it

And, although we try to refine it, we all prolifically stand behind it...

Without even knowing its path and where it's taking us, making us

and most of the time, breaking us.

Unless you're blessed, to have caught the lucky one

I oblige, you can contest. But hear me out

The L-O-V-E can get the hell away from me

But you can get your tell on to me, about your experience

I don't object to hearing it. But I'm subject to fearing it.

Fuck it...

Lay it on me thick, I wanna feel this shit

And at the same time KILL this shit

It's an inner battle, tangent status as I ramble.

They love telling me about love...

Hell, love is real but some make it cheap

Love is sealed but some make it cheat

Some keep it real, while some like to creep

Misleading... Deceiving...Underachieving...

Good grief. Gimme relief. Make your explanation brief.

I hear you...But...

You frontin' on your social networks, you ain't fooling me

Regardless of your likes, status changes and "thirst" looks,

You ain't ruling she or he

Regardless of the follower count, and weekends out

You never know what might be

Hiding behind that phone unlock code

2-5-4-3

whispered erotic tales

Get it W.E.T

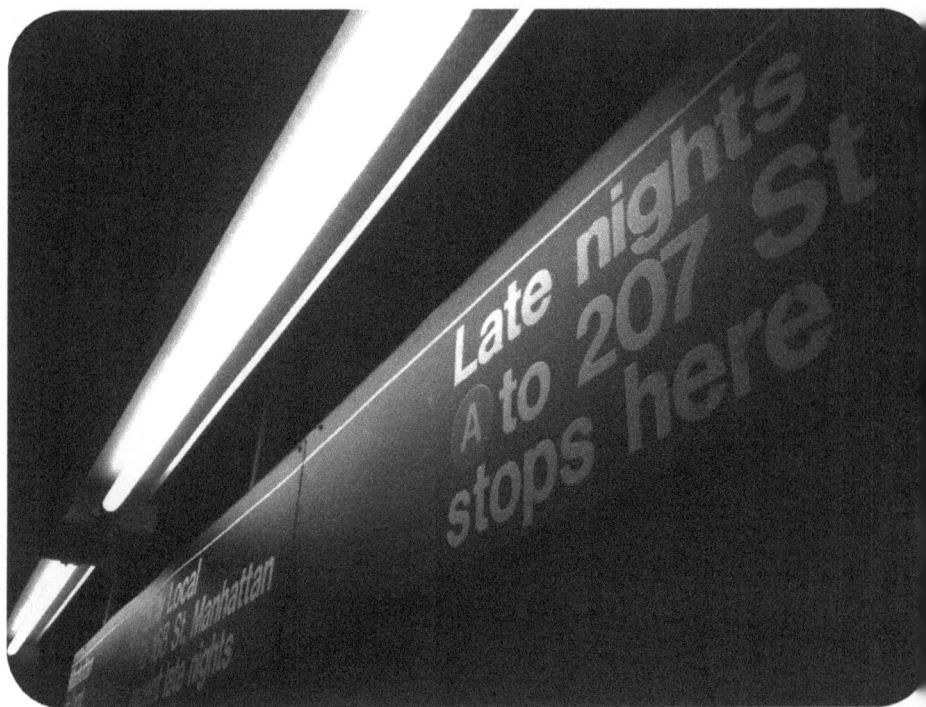

A-TRAIN FANTASY

Let my imagination make love to your ears

Let go of all you have inside, control your biggest fears

I am here.

Just give me one kiss, one night

One bliss, I'll do you right

Loan me your deepest fantasies

I'll give them back true

No limit to your dream of reality, I'll do what you feen me to do

Close your eyes, don't run from me, but circle around your lust

Don't be surprised, just come with me

Let my actions earn your trust

Let me taste your skin, your inhibitions, become unstuck

Let me take you in, I don't mind thrust while I suck

Place your hands on me, touch where ever you want to touch

Open your mouth, speak to me, say naughty things and such

Let me sit on top of you, before he comes to hide

Let me thrust and grind on you, before you come inside

Let me kiss your lips, before you get to mine

Let me pull my hips, up above your eyes

Let my juices drip, as you use your lips, and you taste

My eyes roll, I look down on you, I am sitting on your face

You take in all I give, not letting a drop go to waste

As I come to shiver and quiver, my body is up in space

I slide down, eyes lock on you, I feen you in my place

Your mind no longer running from me, my touch has won the chase

I kiss and gently bite your neck

Our bodies are compressed with our sweat

Your body is in position, I shift it

My mouth feens attention, to your E-Quip-Ment

My mouth move slow, as I tip it

Touch so soft, I like to sip it

Your stretched, your prepared to give it

Letting your aggression control the con-di-tions

Putting my body in a contortionist position

With close precision you slide in

Each wet stroke and smooth glide

So good, I feel sensations in my eyes

But you stop, pull out, I almost said –

But you covered my mouth, moved your head, between my legs

Every cuss word, moan, and "emmm" comes out my mouth

You man handle me, move back inside

Quiet verbiage becomes a shout

But I wake, snap out of it, some moisture out of me

I've experienced this bliss engagement, in my A-Train fantasy.

Next Stop...

DRUNKEN MIXOLOGY

Down your throat, it coats

Absorbing the perimeter with its poison

As I stagger to keep my poise and

Remove my clothes, my body's exposed

But I'm not embarrassed, I'm ready to share this

There you go…wrap your lips around the rim

Lights on dim, my mouth around yours, while my tongue explores

The shaft of your cylinder,

You haven't even touched her yet, and you killin' her

She leaks…

An elixir with the ingredients of a mixer

Temperature warm, brewing climax in its pitcher

I want you to sip her, taste test

Add a little more, tip another pour, take this

Down your throat, it coats

Absorbing the perimeter with its poison

While I'm making the most noise and

Whispering, "oh shit" as your slithering to the clit

Don't you dare spit, unless it's what you wanna do to me in my ear

Come here…

I wrap my legs around your emotions

And feel you deeper with each stroke and, my body's floatin'

You're completely soaked in, my drink, and it's potent

Feeling this con"COCK"tion , I'm zonin'

This could lead to rehab, I'm stonin'

Fuck it, have one more drink, put it on my tab

Here we go again…I'm floatin'

Down your throat, it coats

Absorbing the perimeter with its poison.

LEAK

Wasn't really too thirsty, but didn't mind a little quench

Hydrated how they word me, unexpected moisture in the mix

DRIP...

A little reposition in location

Didn't know what I had in store

Never mind salvaging an already damaged rapport

Not mine, walked in the building saw faces of our kind

One real familiar... soccer? Not gonna play that game

But I was familiar with his name

Especially since it was the same

Yes mine, my heartbeat skipped 2 jumps

Home-girl gravitated, he already knows what he wants

Separated, played my role, did my part

Moderated, in control, from the start

He said, "Nice to meet you," shook my hand, I missed that

opportunity that knocked

But it rang my phone next, broke the barrier that blocked

DRIP…

Entered the room conversation cool vibe

What to do, no intensions to the pipe

But I'll admit, I had a drain needing maintenance to manage

A leak, but not from any exterior type damage

DRIP…DRIP…

I guess I didn't really know what it really was…

Entourage instigating an anticipated massage

I knew he knew, I wasn't a damn masseuse

Elevator talk.. slow walk, a quarter to the deuce

I had a curfew… Shit

DRIP… DRIP… DRIP…

Champagne on deck, cold lotion for the rub

Cork pop help, still didn't know what it really was

Sip sip, DRIP DROP, stop, exchange a kiss, taste this, did he know I

had a crush?

Course not, he had a situation, so he forced the trust with each thrust

Promise me....

Okay...

Promise me...

Okay..

Promise me... You say it...

I promise...

Don't play me...

Deep inside, no DEEP inside he slay me

DRIIIIIP DROP...

Passion in the sheets, no relaxin' to this beat

Music playing, to the pussy slaying

Slip n sliding while I'm dick riding

Don't let the fuck passion fool you

Sensual love-making kisses, firm grips while he do u

Shit talking while he's clit stalking

He said, "How else do you want it?"

Let me jump back on it,

Up in down, he likes it slow

He said "play with your clit"

I said, "you already know"

Eye contact, "How else do you want it?"

He said, "Hold on to my neck."

I said, "I'm already on it."

Mid air, bounce, DRIP, no fuck that, GUSH

Thrusting, tighter grip with each and every push

Legs spread, wrapped around his masculinity

To the couch, back drop, he stroke and glide my femininity

GUSH, SPLASH, never felt this type of thunder

Pushed past any type of other wonder

Back to the bed, we collide our bodies plundered

Back to the position I wanted my body under

He said "How many times did you cum?" As he spanked the ass

I said "Twice."

He said. "Come for me one more time, then I'm gonna cum last."

The final drizzle began pouring...

We're foreign. I knew I wanted more and...DRIP DROP SPLASH.

MILE HIGH CLUB

No first class status

Seats 49a and b

Wishing I was in an apparatus

Placed my bag on top of the seat

No space in the upper head cabin

Placed the carry on between my feet

Thinking back to what had happened

Our bodies are still in heat

He leaned over to adjust my strap, and I pushed the button to raise

his seat,

And even though climax had previously happened

Something still just felt incomplete

Just as we approached our cruising altitude

I'd say about 29, 000 feet

Something came over the both of us

Our arms both began to reach

Stroking, rubbing, touching, the rhythm was right on beat

Then the flight attendant approached us, "Would u like something to drink?"

I said, "I'll take a ginger ale."

He said, "I'll have something to eat."

I mumbled "I got something u can taste…"

She said, "No hot food but here's a treat."

She dropped the peanuts on the tray table

He whispered, "what did u mumble to me?

Cause you know I'll eat u right on this plane, sitting right here in this seat."

Red eye status, most were asleep from what we could see

He said, "Ima head to the lavatory, get up 3 minutes after me."

Headphones in my ear, Maxwell volume low, on repeat

Snatched that shit out my ears, ready for my sneaky retreat

Made my way to the door, all the way on a super creep

Knocked once, door unlocked, pulled me in, the juices began to leak

No time to waste, very little space

But he put his mouth all over me,

I unzipped his pants, he put it in fast

Our adrenaline was pumping to a beat

Of our hearts that raced, we're kissing face to face

I'm pinned tight, I'm up against the sink

We felt the turbulence shake, but this was from OUR own quake

Making love, he stroked my emotions deep

He said, "Let me turn you around, don't u dare make a sound

Grip onto the mirror, not even a peep."

I couldn't take it any longer, sensations getting stronger

I quivered, a little moan came out of me

Watching him have me in the mirror

That quickly became less clearer

Were fogging up this space with our steam

He said, "Oh shit here I come," then we got back to level one

Pulled it back together, it all felt like a dream

We took a quick moment to laugh

He grabbed a chunk of my ass

Couldn't help but unleash our inner freaks

Creeped back out the lav

They don't have what we have

Holding hands we made it back to our seats.

F#%K

So, tip your glass a little further get the liquor in the flesh

You're the cook I'm the server, put this body to the test

No love making tonight..

So don't try your luck,

We bout to…

This pussy as you word her, don't give a fuck about the rest.

Tongue circles on the breast, make a mess, I suggest

Don't contest… I'm winning with your flesh in my flesh

No cup-cakin' tonight,

You game or what?

We bout to…

Bite, nip, suck, while u whisper, "It's the best."

Pull, push, thrust, feel your thunder up my chest

Slipped out, push in, feel it **soakin' wet.**

Nothing will be the same tonight

Lick or suck

We bout to…

Position has been met,

The level has been set,

Drenched in our sweat,

We did it nonetheless,

We fucked.

Now Breathe.

About The Author

TNLMNQ

Tnel Moniq (Tenelle Monique), is an independent video director and editor based in Las Vegas, NV by way of Los Angeles, CA. She is co-founder of Twenty Twenty Vizion Creative Group, which specializes in digital media production. When she isn't shooting music videos and promos, you can find her shooting documentaries for Jay Z's lifeandtimes.com. She continues to write poetic stories and poems about past, present and future life experiences.

Tnel Moniq
WWW.TNELMONIQ.COM

Twenty Twenty Vizion Creative Group
WWW.TWENTYTV.COM

Instagram: tnelmoniq

Twitter: @tnelmoniq
Email: tnel@twentytv.com

www.ingramcontent.com/pod-product-compliance
Lightning Source LLC
Chambersburg PA
CBHW060201070426
42447CB00033B/2260